NEW TOWNS AFTER THE WAR

NEW VISTAS

War from the city sky has brought not only destruction, but light and a wid
vision. Can we retain these gifts when we rebuild?

NEW TOWNS
AFTER THE WAR

By

F. J. OSBORN

LONDON

J. M. DENT AND SONS LTD.

CONTENTS

ILLUSTRATIONS

PREFACE TO THE 1942 EDITION

I WROTE the first edition of this little book in 1918 in consultation with Ebenezer Howard, C. B. Purdom, and W. G. Taylor. Messrs Dent published it out of a patriotic desire to prepare the way for the planning of a better Britain. The book received short but cordial reviews in the small number of papers which at that time did not regard planning and town-building as a long-haired eccentricity. Apart from these I never had the slightest direct evidence that any responsible person read it except Mr Bernard Shaw (of whom more later) and the three friends named who suggested it and kept me up to the scratch in writing it. Nevertheless, it must have had some effect, because in 1919 there was a certain amount of discussion of the possibility of building a number of new towns as part of the coming housing drive—which by then was developing great impetus under the attractive slogan 'Homes for Heroes.'

In fact there was sufficient response to encourage the four of us to start a New Towns Group, and Purdom and I wrote articles in popular papers, lobbied political parties, and toured mayoral parlours in an endeavour to get the Government and the great municipalities to translate our very practical proposals into action. I must add that Ebenezer Howard, while delighted at our youthful yet realistic restatements of his ideas, showed a doubt about our strategy which puzzled me at the time. He used to see me off on my missionary tours with comforting words like these: 'My dear boy, I hope you have a pleasant trip; but you are wasting your time. If you wait for the

7

authorities to build new towns you will be older than Methuselah before they start. The only way to get anything done is to do it yourself.'

To the rest of us this was unacceptable advice. We had all taken minor parts in building the First Garden City founded by Howard at Letchworth. We considered that the practicability of building new towns had been shown—as indeed it had, beyond all cavil. We did not think another mere demonstration, another trial model, was necessary. We wanted the idea applied in all the regions of Britain as a national policy. I had put it very clearly in this little book that unless it were applied as a national policy, the great housing endeavour would go all wrong—we should just get vast new suburban additions to cities already far too large. And that, of course, is what actually happened. Anybody can see it now. I think it can be fairly said that we four were, if not the only people in Britain who saw it in 1918 and 1919, at least the only group that persistently and clearly pointed out the danger and the opportunity.

We kept it up for quite a time, tiresomely nagging at Whitehall and the municipal corporations, at the political parties, and through the Press at the public. I cannot speak for the others, but I confess that as the months passed I felt more and more like Max Beerbohm's caricature of Walt Whitman inciting the American Eagle to soar. Nevertheless, despite a fair amount of political experience, I clung to an obstinate belief that consistent and intelligent argument tells. My instinct was to go on badgering everybody until either they did what we suggested, or some principal secretary or speculative builder put a bullet through me.

Whether this instinct was right or wrong I don't know, and I shall never find out. For one day in 1919, when I came back from lecturing in the north, Howard met me at a London terminus with news that brought me down with a bump to solid earth—four square miles of it. The story has often been told, but never adequately; indeed, to do justice to it would require the scope of a novelist and the technique of a historian. Very briefly, Howard, then a man of seventy-one, had grown tired of our pathetic pleadings to authority to act imaginatively on a large scale; and without consultation with the younger three-quarters of the New Towns Group had been off to an auction sale and bought a large part of the site for a second garden city off his own bat! I was not present when he broke this story to Purdom and Taylor, but I can remember my own reactions very clearly; I was speechless with admiration and baffled rage. Admiration, because like most planning-minded people I tend to defer action for the perfect opportunity which never comes, and therefore always feel the superiority of people who cut knots and do things; rage because I knew that the initiation of another garden city by private enterprise was just the get-out that the authorities, slightly bothered by public response to our propaganda, would jump at. (And they did.) Admiration and rage were blended too when I studied the pretty trap in which that wonderful old man had caught his disciples.

Think of our position. Howard was the world-re-nowned founder of the garden city movement; not only the symbol we raised and threw our little spotlights on, but so essentially sound, and so single-minded and dis-interested, that it was out of the question for us to re-pudiate him or let him down. It was impossible to trim our sails. If he was only twenty-five per cent of the party, he was ninety-nine per cent of the international garden city movement. We had to accept his *fait accompli* or retire into complete futility from a campaign that had become part of our lives. He had not only burnt his boats; he had burnt ours; and I am sure he inwardly chuckled at the situation, having no sense of self-preservation when great public issues were at stake. The most extraordinary feature of his exploit is that he had bought the land without enough money to pay even the deposit of ten per cent to the auctioneer who sold it. He had hurriedly rushed round to a few people who believed in him and had a touch of the heroic themselves (G. G. Blane, J. R. Farquharson, F. E. Fremantle, R. L. Reiss, and Franklin Thomasson were among these) and borrowed a few thousands; and, as the money so collected fell short of the amount of the necessary deposit, he seemed to have no difficulty in persuading the agent who bought it for him at the sale to fork out the deficiency —though this agent, Mr Norman Savill, was not at that time in the least interested in the garden city movement. Mr Savill, whom we got to know well afterwards, is a surveyor of exceptional foresight and imagination; but he belongs to one of the most hard-boiled of the professions, and no one but Howard would ever have induced an agent to do such a thing.

That was the beginning of the history of Welwyn Garden City. There were many other circumstances which at that time made the whole enterprise seem to me utterly crazy and impracticable. For example, the land Howard bought at that auction, though ideal in situation and character for the nucleus of a new town, was useless for the purpose without the addition of a very large area of adjoining land belonging to an owner, the present Marquess of Salisbury, who had no thought whatever of selling it. And in all common sense that should (as I said at once) have killed the scheme before its birth. But Lord Salisbury was at that time, by a lucky coincidence, President of the Garden Cities Association—and it is fair to say that, while really not desiring the building of a

new town in just that position, he found himself in much
the same fix as Howard's own colleagues. Howard
shamelessly played upon his lordship's great sense of
public duty. And he came into line very handsomely
and under much less compulsion, selling the necessary
land at the most modest estimate of its value.

There is not space to tell of the other almost insuperable
obstacles, nor of how they were overcome and the new
town brought to birth, nursed, reared, and finally weaned
as the vigorous and prosperous industrial community
that it is to-day. The four New Townsmen, who set out
to persuade Britain to build one hundred new towns,
found instead that for a large part of their lives they were
to participate in the building of one new town. Purdom
became Finance Director and perhaps the biggest driving
force in the early stages of development. I had a most
interesting and educational experience as estate manager,
publicist, and industrial bagman for the town, doubling
such functions for a time with those of clerk, finance and
rating officer of the local authority. Taylor went early
to live in the town and took a valuable part in its civic
and cultural life. And Howard was almost the first
resident of the town, threw himself into all its activities,
died there, as Sir Ebenezer Howard, in 1928, and has his
memorial in the main street, which bears his name. The
rest of the tiny group subsequently had differences of
opinion between themselves and with the Board of Directors of Welwyn Garden City, and none of them is now
officially connected with the scheme. But that is another
story, of relatively little interest. My purpose in this
note has been to record the connection between the book
and the establishment of Howard's Second Garden City and,
perhaps a little ironically, to remind myself and the reader
that things do sometimes happen as a result of thought
and persuasion, but not always exactly what one expects.

The way in which the principles expounded in this book (which were, of course, only a modernization and development of the principles employed in the building of Letchworth, founded by Howard and the strong group associated with him in 1903) were put into practice was described in 1925 by C. B. Purdom in his book *The Building of Satellite Towns*—still a most useful record. Much water has passed down the two little rivers of Welwyn Garden City since then, and even more under the bridges of the Thames. Welwyn is an achievement of which any group might be proud—an industrial town of 20,000 (half-way to its objective of 40,000), healthy, productive in war and peace, and beautiful. But it is only one town, containing between 4,000 and 5,000 houses and perhaps 9,000 or 10,000 workers in its factories and businesses. Between the two wars Great Britain built four *million* houses—nearly a thousand times as many as were built at Welwyn—and a vast number of these, probably quite half, were built in such places that they added to the public waste of time in daily travel, diminished local community life, sprawled disastrously over fields and along main roads, or were crowded together in layers in the detestable form of tenement flats.

Who was right—the practical Howard, or the more intransigent balance of his little group? The case for Howard is that if he had not acted as he did we should have had *no* new town at all instead of *one*. And having got to know my bureaucrats and industrialists more intimately in these twenty odd years I am not sure he was wrong.

Now, however, the circumstances are entirely different. The public is at last planning-conscious. The absurdity of the unlimited expansion of cities by the suburb-plus-rapid-transport method is recognized by all but transport idealists and municipal corporations thinking solely in

terms of rateable value.   Flats remain unpopular with the
masses despite the most persistent propaganda by architectural playboys who want larger boxes of plasticine
with which to indulge their creative fancy.   Town-
dwellers at last realize the importance of agriculture and
consciously desire contact with country life.   No one
defends ribbon-building along main roads.   Even the
idea of skilled control of the external appearance of whole
streets and groups of buildings has gained wide acceptance.   And the Barlow Report has shown that control
of the location of industry, necessary for many social
and strategic reasons, is also in the interests of the
efficiency of industry itself.   To all these changes in
opinion are added the need and the opportunity brought
about by war-destruction and damage.   In 1919 we were
faced with a problem of building expansion and the over-
taking of arrears.   To-day the problem is primarily one
of rebuilding—though there are still arrears to make up.
And we are not any of us so satisfied with our old cities that
we want to rebuild them just as they were.   We have a
chance to replan, and we have a chance to loosen out
congestion, to substitute gracious and healthy surroundings for dark, drab, and debasing streets, tenements, and
slums, to give better working conditions for industry and
greater security for agriculture, to think of the requirements of our people as individuals, as families, as workers,
as citizens, and to shape our cities and protect our countryside in the best interests of all.

The ideas and ideals worked out by the pioneer planners
over the last forty years are still in evolution and must be
continually adapted to economic and social changes.   But
those pioneers did their work well, and certain principles
stand.   They and others are spending what time they
can in working out the adaptation of these principles to
the situation after the second war, so far as it is possible

B

to anticipate it. But there is a vast public which is new to the subject. It is a complex subject—very troublesome to summarize in a manner both sound and easy to grasp. Reading through this little book of mine after twenty-three years I do not think I could much improve upon the statement of the main essentials of planning so far as they affect the ordinary man. I could add a lot in the way of critical analysis of the structure of the old cities; I could collect together the results of the immense amount of research work which has been done by economists and statisticians in the last few years; I could stud the story with an impressive pattern of brass tacks derived from experience at Welwyn and elsewhere. But that would produce another book altogether, and the picture, if richer and sounder, would be less easy to grasp. I have, therefore, left the little book of 1918 much as it was, deleting a few obsolete references and introducing only such brief allusions to new factors as are necessary to avoid any sense of unreality.

I sent the manuscript of *New Towns After the War* in 1918 to Mr Bernard Shaw, asking him to write a preface for it. He replied at some length, in his own beautiful handwriting, declining to do so, for *my* sake as well as his own, and indeed warning all unknown authors against letting him introduce them to the public. His letter was (though I hadn't the sense to see it at the time) clearly intended to help me in gaining a hearing, and at the same time to be a Shaw preface to end prefaces. I put it away and did not rediscover it until I was preparing this edition. It seemed to me to have great interest as a document in the case, so I wrote him asking his permission to quote it, and sending him a copy of the letter with the draft of this preface. His reply was, as ever, surprising. He refused, on the ground that his old letter was now useless, nothing to do with garden cities, and of no interest to the public. And he wrote into my draft the following:

16th October 1941.

Dear Mr Osborn,

In 1918 I wrote to you that your *New Towns After the War* was the best written and best argued case for garden cities I had read. I am glad to learn that you are bringing out a new edition of it.

I am one of those investors who like to see something for their money instead of merely changing transfers with some old shareholder and adding nothing to the country's fixed capital. I found the new garden cities just what I wanted. I saw waste places changed into pleasant and well planned dwellings and handsome markets by my spare cash. The investments never gave me a moment's anxiety or trouble: they were and are entirely satisfactory, both morally and economically. I am glad I foresaw their future when my neighbours were buying shares in South American railways which are now bankrupt.

I knew Ebenezer Howard personally and mentioned him in my play called *John Bull's Other Island* nearly forty years ago. An amazing man, whom the Stock Exchange would have dismissed as a negligible crank.

Faithfully,

G. Bernard Shaw.

To avoid misunderstanding, I stress the designed limits of this little book. It made in 1918, and makes now, no pretence to cover the whole field of Town and Country Planning, though it is written, I think, in awareness of the whole field. The building of new towns and the planned extension of existing small towns, which is the subject here dealt with, fits into a larger framework of policy on which most of the responsible planners in this country now agree. It is consistent with the policy, recommended by the Barlow Report of 1940, of decentralization from the great towns and a reasonable balance and diversification of industry throughout the country. It is also consistent with the Planning Basis recently drafted by the

Town and Country Planning Association and adopted by such bodies as the Royal Institute of British Architects and the National Council of Social Service. But these programmes contain other matters as well that all planners think important; for example, a continuous survey of national resources, the creation of better regional machinery for planning, and the reservation of national park areas and coastal strips. Town and country planning technique has to deal with the control in detail of building development everywhere. Its elevation to the national scale, which every one now agrees is necessary, raises some difficult (and very interesting) questions of administration, and an intricate problem of land values which is at present being examined by an expert committee presided over by Mr Jusice Uthwatt. For those interested in these other aspects of land-use planning a **very** brief bibliography is given at the end of this book.

Keystone Press Agency Ltd.

A GREAT INDUSTRIAL CITY

The sun is shining, but note the shadows in the streets. The one visible open space, in the centre of the picture, is a recent great improvement. The extreme over-building of factories, commercial buildings, and dwellings is clearly shown. No local rearrangement can give adequate space and light in such a city. It needs a long-term programme for business decentralization and reduction of over-all density.

NEW TOWNS AFTER THE WAR

DURING the second World War, as during the first, the erection of houses and other buildings for civil purposes has practically stopped. Necessarily we are getting into arrears with normal replacement. In addition we have this time the new factor of large-scale bombing, which is depleting our stock of fixed property, especially in the bigger cities. At present all our energies, including those of the much reduced building industry, must be given to war purposes. But the moment the war is over the building industry, and all the industries which make materials, fittings, and furnishings for buildings, must be set energetically to work to make up an unprecedented shortage of every kind of accommodation—houses, shops, offices, warehouses, factories, public buildings. In the organization and finance of this work the State and the other public authorities, every one now agrees, must take a definite lead. But industry has to organize for the work also; and public opinion must understand the issues, because, both in pressure and patience, it will play a decisive part.

The situation at the end of the war will be such that a great national design can, if we will it and are ready, be impressed on the rebuilding programme. The scale of the work to be done makes possible, as indeed it made possible after the last war, a more imaginative and scientific policy of replanning than has ever been attempted. We missed our opportunity last time, though this little book pointed the way to it. It would be unforgivable to miss it again. Every one ought therefore to devote some of his leisure time to thinking about the reconstruction period, should try to understand the vast number of interests and personal wishes that have to be reconciled and co-ordinated in a national policy, and should consider what he or she can do to promote agreement and get ready for prompt action. There should be no deduction from total war effort in this; nor should it be mere recreative day-dreaming (or black-out-dreaming). Realistic planning for the future, if not overdone, may well inspire in us greater energy for the distasteful tasks of the present.

Manufacturers interested in the efficiency of industry, ordinary men and women wanting better surroundings for life and work, agriculturists seeking a revivification of the countryside, parents and educationists concerned for the well-being of the young, indeed, all who desire the bodily, social, and aesthetic health of the nation, are asked to weigh without prejudice the argument of this book. It does not pretend to cover more than one aspect of the vast problem of Reconstruction, even of physical reconstruction, but it does make proposals which relate to many other aspects, and can be fitted into the larger policy. The proposals, when made in 1918, seemed very bold; by many people they were thought extravagant and unreal, and to some they will seem so to-day. But examination will show them to be perfectly feasible, and to involve no departure from precedent save in the single aspect of the scale in which they are conceived, which, however, is by no means out of proportion to the need and the opportunity.

THE OPPORTUNITY

HOUSING has always had its difficulties since the time of primitive man, whose cave was dark, insanitary, and ill fitted. But the housing problem as it is known to the modern world, especially in Great Britain and America, originated as a characteristic feature of the industrial revolution and the rapid crowding of the population in towns. It is a problem which has never at any time been effectually dealt with. The advances of the nineteenth century in sanitary science, housing legislation, and ideas of public health seem in retrospect to mark stages in the gradual realization of housing evils rather than positive successes in grappling with them. Criticism outpaced action; and the problem itself developed faster than either. Up to the last war the twentieth century had no better record to show. Housing remained hopelessly bad and inadequate. Between the two wars Great Britain made an immense effort to deal with its housing arrears. We built no less than four million houses in that period. But eight million dwellings still survive from before 1914, the majority of which are incompetently designed, unsoundly built, and in various ways destructive of the health and comfort of their occupants. And even in 1939 there were still not enough of them to go round: if every dwelling, good or bad, had then been occupied, the number fell short of the need by hundreds of thousands.

Of the four million houses built between the wars, about one million were provided by local authorities under the Housing Acts. Thus the provision of houses has still been mainly in the hands of private agencies. On some great town estates and in the country ground landlords have built houses; a few employers have housed their own workers; and public utility societies, encouraged by loans under the Housing Acts, have taken a part important rather for the lead in design and quality they have given them than for the magnitude of their contribution. The great majority of houses have been produced by the speculative builders or by private contract, very largely for occupying owners who have obtained finance for their purchases through building societies, and to a less extent through loans from local authorities. Many of these houses, originally acquired by their occupiers, have been sold to investment companies and let on rental. While therefore the proportion of houses provided by public activity and with the aid of State capital increased very much between the two wars, it still remained true that the great bulk of house-building was the work of private agencies. These agencies, however, never succeeded in producing houses at rents within the means of the lower-paid workers. Increasingly the public effort directed its attention to this part of the demand, to meet which substantial subsidies were necessary. Though standards of new construction had to be progressively lowered in the effort to bridge the gap between rental and the ability to pay, the problem of housing the lower-paid workers was never fully solved, and too many of this group continued, and still continue, to live in worn-out slums or the subdivided cast-off houses of the higher income groups.

Thus there were still serious arrears of housing in 1939. How far the shortage will have been accentuated during the war by bombing destruction cannot at present be estimated. The guess may, however, be hazarded that the necessary building effort in the reconstruction period

after this war will not be less than it was after the last
war. This may be true of housing alone. When we add
the replacement of factories, offices, shops, and public
buildings destroyed by bombing, the total effort required
will probably much exceed that of the last reconstruction
period. And the urgency of replacement, and the con-
sequent factor of expansion of the building industry, is
likely to be even greater. Indeed, it may be anticipated
that it will require, for a period of ten years, the utmost
extension of the building industry, and of the building
supplies industry, of which the nation is capable.

While speed and efficiency alike will prompt us to make
the greatest possible use of the initiative and organizing
power of private firms and persons, it is clear that the
State and the local authorities will have to play a much
larger part in the organization of all this work than in the
past. In the nature of the case there will be pressure
from every area and every interest for the maximum
speed of replacement. That raises at once questions of
priority and of competition for supplies and contracts
which only the State can settle or adjust. There are also
vast and socially important issues of man power and
training, not only in the building industry, but in all the
ancillary industries. And if the interests of the ordinary
wage-earning house-dweller are to be regarded, there will
be acute problems of finance and of housing subsidies.
Priorities in finance, as well as in materials and building
services, have to be decided. It is obvious that these
must be subject to national policy if we are not to have a
grossly distorted building effort.

This affords a unique opportunity for the nation to
deal with the whole question of rebuilding in a bold and
imaginative way. Building is to be undertaken on a
larger scale than ever before, and with an unprecedented
degree of central control. Political conditions will be

highly favourable to extensive measures. What follows is a suggestion for a national plan. The intimate relations between housing and other matters of present public concern will be shown; and an attempt will be made to sketch out broadly a policy commensurate with the needs of the time.

THE PROBLEM

THE difficulty of which most people were conscious after the last war was that the number of dwellings was grossly insufficient. To this we now add a greater consciousness of poor design and scanty equipment. But in dealing with these immediate problems we should not overlook the larger difficulty that stands behind them, which is that most of the dwellings we now possess are in the wrong places. Houses are significantly permanent objects in a world of changing ideas and wants. The replacing of old houses by new, calling not only for hard work but for the sacrifice of tangible property and sentimental associations, is in the nature of a revolution—and revolutions are always late. Even if it is possible to get rid of an undesirable house, that does not dispose of the vested interest in the ground rent. Once a building site always a building site; or so it seems. Once land is developed, no matter how badly, it is all but impossible to turn it back into agricultural land.

Our great towns seem to be imperishable memorials to our ancestors' lack of foresight. Many streets are too narrow; houses, factories, and shops are crowded together in an inconvenient and unhealthy jumble; and yet in ninety-nine cases out of a hundred, when the buildings wear out, we replace them by loftier buildings occupying much the same area and perpetuating the old plan which every one will admit to be indefensible. It is true that when the value of a site happens to rise, rebuilding may be hastened in the interest of a more intensive cultivation of the ground-rental possibilities; but when the site value goes down, the old building is not rebuilt if the owner can help it; it remains in use so long as a shilling a week profit can be got from it, or until the sanitary authority mercifully intervenes with a demolition order. Even then the problem is by no means disposed of, but enters into a new phase. The site may be left derelict, like a gap in a row of bad teeth. More likely another structure will be built in its place to perplex the sociologists of a century later.

This uncanny tenacity of building sites ought to make us think very hard about the position of every house before we build it; and in that cogitation not only the prospective owner is concerned. It is very slowly being realized that housing has close connections with many other matters of social interest; with public health, with transport, with the problems of industrial and agricultural organization, with child welfare and education, with national and local government, and with every aspect of the civic and cultural life of the community. We have left this branch of activity almost wholly to the landjobber and the speculative builder, who do not and cannot take any account of its infinite social ramifications. Housing is a matter in which collective foresight and collective design are essential. But only in structural details of individual buildings has social control been exercised; and even in these matters we have as yet hardly done more than what was imperative in order to avoid the threat of epidemics.

TOWN PLANNING NOT ENOUGH

The gradual adoption of the Town and Country Planning Acts marks a recognition of the necessity of design locally. But we have still to grasp that the issues

London News Agency Photos Ltd.

THREE WAYS OF HOUSING

bove). Stepney: Gardenless terrace-houses, giving place to five-story
ements. (*Below*). Terrace-houses with open front gardens in the new
town of Welwyn Garden City.

tects: C. M. Hennell & C. H. James, F.R.I.B.A. Studio Lisa

with which housing is bound up are wider than the borders of the town, and that a truly effective design must be national in its scope. A substantial revival of agriculture, for example, will affect town development as well as countryside development. The adoption of the most enlightened town-plan for one expanding great city will not be of much use to the declining country town. The spread of a great city over a few more counties may be a source of pride to its lord mayor and corporation, and yet disastrous to the nation as a whole.

Before the war [1] we were as far as ever from grappling with the fundamental question of the extent and distribution of towns in relation to rural areas. We were treating symptoms rather than the general complex of diseases. The tendency of our great towns to grow vigorously but injudiciously on the edges, while deteriorating towards the centre, was very inadequately met by sanitary laws, building regulations, and timid town-planning schemes. The workers near the centre were crowded in tenements — tall, inhuman barracks with narrow paved yards—or, even worse, in the subdivided rooms of houses abandoned by the prosperous. Suburban development of a poor type, consisting of long rows of maisonettes without beauty or variety, packed together in order to extract the maximum profit from their sites, was all too common. And even where, as in many of the municipal housing estates, the houses were good, and well spaced, they were often too far from shopping centres and places of work.

[1] The original reference was to 1914. The statement remains true when 1939 is substituted

THE DIAGNOSIS INADEQUATE

Our attempts to deal with these evils were not only too minute in scope, but based on too narrow a diagnosis to effect much improvement. Rural housing was suffering from the same limitation of treatment. The agricultural workers were living in the crumbling hovels of past generations, and most of the villages and many of the country towns were declining. A great deal of anxiety was expressed as to the effect of bad housing, whether urban or rural, upon the health, efficiency, and political docility of the workers. But what dwarfed everything else in apparent urgency was that even of the types of accommodation existing, nothing like a sufficiency was obtainable. The accentuation of the shortage by bombing may hustle us again into a short-sighted policy. In the desperate necessity of building dwellings of some sort in large quantities immediately peace returns we may be tempted to ignore the major defects of our housing system. And to ignore them is to enlarge them—to put further obstacles in the way of a later more resolute and inspired generation.

THE URBAN DISEASE

Like the error in the distribution of wealth, the enormous error in the distribution of houses about the country is a fact almost too large to grasp, and one which the practical man therefore often finds it convenient to ignore. The census figures are familiar enough; we have so often been told that the majority of the people of England live in the great towns, and only a small proportion in the small towns and in the country, that we can no longer receive the information with a healthy surprise. We ought to be shocked at the news that Scotland, with an area of 30,000 square miles, has a population about equal to that of the County of London, with an area of 120 square miles; and that more than a quarter of this population lives in the one city of Glasgow. But we have lost a healthy capacity to be shocked by such facts. We ought to be even more shocked that twenty-five per cent of the population of Great Britain was concentrated into London and the Home Counties in 1937, as compared with eighteen per cent in 1801, and that just before this war nearly half the population were living in the twenty largest urban agglomerations, and a third of them in six of those agglomerations. The figures are stale; they bore us. Nevertheless, the evil effects of this mal-distribution continue and intensify. Though our most respected and far-sighted men have warned us for genera-tions of the dangers and disadvantages of the over-growth of the larger towns and the depopulation of others and of the countryside, the process has been allowed to go on without check.

Even the town-planning movement, having little hope of damming the stream towards the larger cities, has so far limited itself in practice to the better arrangement of suburbs. 'The duty of the housing expert and of the city plannner alike is to see to it that the city population of the future, when it is twice as large as at present—a time less than thirty years off—is spread over more than twice the area of the present city.' This assumption of an American city planner in 1914 may be said to have been the key-note of inter-war planning. The policy which it summarizes is based on a misunderstanding of the case against the great city.

It is beyond all question that the great city throughout history has been inimical to life and health. The statis-tics, particularly of infant mortality, show this. But even more conclusive is the simple evidence of the different appearance of children living under city and country conditions at comparable levels of family income. Not only by its overcrowding, which if avoidable has never yet been avoided, but by its vitiated atmosphere, by the lack of sun and vegetation in and about its houses, by its crowded underground transport, by its dusty streets, by its numerous cramped and unhealthy factories, offices, and workshops, by its far-carried supplies of milk and perishable foods, by the facilities it offers to infectious diseases, by its inadequate play-space for children and adults—in all these ways the great city has killed and weakened its citizens by multitudes. For decades it subsisted on the physical vitality which was recruited in the country districts. Considered historically, its drain upon the racial life has been comparable with that of war.

DIFFICULTIES OF CITY REFORM

Let us agree that the killing power of the great city has been much reduced in the last fifty years. By means of sanitation, planning of new extensions, public health measures, slum clearance, child welfare services, etc., great improvements in health have been achieved. Yet there is a limit to this improvement if the size and structure of the great city remain unchanged. The freshness of a given quantity of air is reduced in proportion to the number of human beings who breathe it. Smoke is not likely to be abolished from domestic heating for many years. Nor is an effective dilution of the housing density of central areas a practicable policy, unless we can achieve the partial dispersal of the business and industry which is their core. An intense concentration in the centre is a characteristic of their economic structure. Ill-considered or unplanned interference with that concentration would be like breaking the tail of a Prince Rupert's drop; it

THE ARCHITECTURAL FLAT

Certainly it is magnificent.   But is it a right environment for family life fr
childhood to old age?

would upset the balance of cohesions and tensions, and the whole thing would go to pieces. This indeed can happen without interference, by the spontaneous movement of industry from the city centre.

THE ECONOMIC DEFECTS OF THE CITY

The great city is not an economically efficient type of organization in modern circumstances, quite apart from the factor of health in which it is unequivocally condemned. Beyond a certain stage of growth it certainly wastes more social effort than it saves. It is certainly a highly concentrated market and labour-supply for industries centrally placed; but these advantages are offset by the high rents and high wages which such industries must cover. The centralization of finance and commerce is, in these days of the telegraph, telephone, cheap postage, and highly developed banking systems, far less valuable than it was. The two or three hours per day spent by industrial and business workers in travelling to and from their homes is economic waste. The congestion of buildings on the land severely limits the amount of house accommodation for each family. The workers benefit little if at all by the higher wages, because these are nullified by travelling expenses and town prices. When we take into account the quantities of land, house-room, and leisure left to the town worker as a reward for his exertions, it is arguable that urban ground values are the result more of an extortion of effort than of any real saving by association.

THE SOCIAL DEFECTS OF THE CITY

Socially and culturally the great city has less to commend it than is commonly assumed. Its artistic and

c

political activities are confined to tiny minority groups, the mass of inhabitants being deprived of the capacity for culture by the conditions of their lives. The great city is without design, for the most part dirty, noisy, and ugly, and remote from the basic processes of nature which are as necessary for aesthetic as for physical health. It is so large and unwieldy that civic sense, if it exists, is lopped and warped. Hence it is weak in traditions or ideals. Its inevitable divisions into working and dormitory districts make its local politics confused and unrepresentative, and not only local but national democracy is thereby impoverished in truly representative personalities.

The case against the great city can be endlessly elaborated, and only a short summary is possible here. But particular attention should be paid to the fact that the maladies above described are complementary to those of the rural districts and the smaller towns.

THE DISEASE OF THE COUNTRYSIDE

For many years not only our villages, but most of our small towns, declined in vitality. The new things, the popular excitements, the sense of power and progress, all seemed to centre in the cities, where the streets were full of people and newspapers were issued ten times a day. The villages were voted dull, and their smallness and isolation made social tyranny almost inevitable. For the rural worker's life is a life without suitable alternatives. There is generally only one cottage in which he can live, only one school to which he can send his children, only one employer for whom he can work, and so on. Without alternatives there can be no sense of freedom. And the monotony of village life is not relieved by adequate chances for the worker to attain a position of independence and security, or to fulfil reasonable ambitions for himself or for his family.

Many country towns are stagnant. They fulfil their waning functions in relation to the villages, but they are not conscious of that current of creative activity which is a need of the enterprising and vigorous. This is not surprising when we reflect that the number of workers employed in the agricultural industry on which these towns are based has fallen steadily for half a century. But it is doubtful if the decline stands in relation to the slump in agricultural profits as a simple case of effect and cause. Agriculture is not so unprofitable as all that, and it is far from certain that a mere reversal of the economic engine by means of bonuses, minimum wages, and subsidized rural housing will fully counteract the present tendencies. Even a revolution in land tenure might not do so. There is a psychological element in the process of decline which these proposals do little or nothing to deal with. The sense that a village or small town is a promising place for alert-minded people will be very hard to restore.

CONTRAST BETWEEN TOWN AND COUNTRY

On the other hand, the great industrial towns and town-tracts, unhealthy, hideous, and inimical to the graces of civilization as they are, simply boil over with the vitality which is so sadly to seek in the rural areas. Business is variegated and enterprising. Trade unions are occasionally aggressive. Co-operation and antagonism are organized in a thousand interesting forms. Amusements and distractions clamour to be enjoyed. Politics and movements, though mass-produced and more and more assimilated to commercial advertising technique, are noisy and have popular entertainment value. Be it illusion or reality, there is a feeling that things are on move, that to-morrow may be different from to-day, that anything may happen to anybody.

This tends to become less true of the very big towns, since the advancing edge is out of touch with the centre, where slum-dwellers can be found with the same dull boredom at the lack of change and development which marks the villager. But it still looks true to the young rural worker who wants lively surroundings and adventure, and it is true enough to deter him from returning to the village.

The contrast between town and country is altogether too extreme to be masked by rural reform alone. Even if housing were improved, small holdings and allotments created, and village culture stimulated; even if the demand for labour in the country were increased while the demand in the towns fell off, there would still be a tendency for some of the best of the younger countrymen to migrate to the cities. There they would have little difficulty in getting work, since they would replace the less vigorous town workers, who would not take their places in the country, but would sink into the semi-destitute class characteristic of urban areas.

Why do Great Towns continue to Grow?

The workers drift into the city primarily because jobs are more easily found there. Obviously they could not, in the long run, maintain themselves there unless the urban industries expanded also. But the industries go to the towns because they are vast pools of labour and selling markets at the same time. New factories are continually being built in and around the great towns, and new houses put up for the growing population. It is a vicious circle. Labour goes to the cities because industry is expanding there. Industry expands in the cities because labour is plentiful there. Public policy in housing and services not only follows but also anticipates and stimulates the cityward trend.

Good economic and historical causes can be traced for the original impetus of every city's growth; but these original causes have in many cases ceased to hold good. As the building area has extended, the increase in the cost of production caused by excessive internal transport, dear rents, and high nominal wages, must often have reached a figure which would pay for the distribution of the raw materials over a much wider area. Here we come upon the paradoxical effect of improved transport facilities. Up to a certain point cities grew about particular centres through the combined forces of economic advantage and molecular attraction. The acceleration of transport enabled such cities to grow to an uneconomic size before any one noticed that the same development would have permitted a movement of industry and population in very different directions.

We are far from comprehending even yet that urban concentration means a measureless amount of transportation of citizens and goods within the city; whereas relative diffusion would mean the transportation merely of a few raw materials and finished products—over longer distances, certainly, on the average, but with a far smaller total expenditure of energy.

This is true of towns in the coal areas; and it is to some extent true even of those which cluster about the chief seaports. Above all, it is true of London and of other cities whose historic origin was rather political than industrial.

No Well-equipped Small Towns

Why, then, has industry continued to go to these great towns?

For two reasons. First, because they are immense reservoirs of every kind of labour. Second, because there has been nowhere else for industry to go. The rural areas have not catered for its needs. The enterprising manufacturer is hesitant to place his new factory in a country town which is obviously and even consciously on the down grade, even if such a town could provide the space, power, and other facilities required. He cannot, unless he is in a very large way of business, build a village for himself. (There are, in any case, grave social objections to such 'tied' villages.) A well-equipped and vigorous small town would for many industries have all the economic arguments as against a great city. But there are hardly any such small towns. The old country towns grew up when industrial conditions were altogether different from those of to-day. They are not adapted to modern needs; and without immense effort and an expenditure beyond their own resources, they cannot offer what industry requires.

The Decentralization of Industry

The manner in which industry has sought in the last forty years to combine the facilities and labour-reserve of the town with the advantages of cheap land is curious. It has spread itself along the main lines of communication just outside the urban centres. The workers live in the town or the outlying suburbs and travel by train to their work. In some cases a new subsidiary centre grows up, and many of the economic advantages of the small town are thus attained for the time being.

But, unfortunately, there is no limit to the growth of the subsidiary centres, and the new urban area expands until it coalesces with the main city as a continuous built-up agglomeration. Other industries, large enough to pump their own water and make their own power, spread still farther out along the radial railway, road, and canal routes. This tendency is very noticeable in the London area, and unless it is controlled will transform the Home Counties into a congeries of large industrial towns. It is thus not really a process of decentralization, but simply a modification of the old centripetal process. Socially it is bad: the city being made more cumbrous, and the amount of transport increased. But it is interesting as showing that the industrial advantages of the great city have little to do with centrality of position, but depend mainly upon transport, power, and the capacity to attract workers.[1]

THE PROCESS WILL CONTINUE

In default of some designed intervention the present development will go on. Industry will continue to drift to and expand in the urban areas, making them even more unhealthy and unwieldy. The attempt to revive agriculture may be more or less successful—that will depend upon the amount of artificial stimulus which the State is prepared to supply—but men and women of spirit will still be reluctant to stay in the rural districts. The vast majority of our children will continue to be born and bred and in large measure killed off in the great cities. The small towns will uninterruptedly decline.

[1] This and the two succeeding paragraphs are exactly as I had them in the 1918 edition. Unhappily, my prophecies came true.

GARDEN SUBURBS AND SLUM CLEARANCES

It is to be noted that all attempts to reform the city internally have the effect of enlarging the urban area. Great advances have been made in suburb planning and the design of small houses, as a result of the experience of municipalities and public utility societies. But new garden suburbs and modern cottages, vastly superior as they are to their predecessors, make cities bigger that are already far too big. The same is true of the slum clearances undertaken by various municipalities, in connection with the driving of new roads or the more spacious planning of crowded districts. These are good and necessary things, but under present circumstances vastly expensive for the town, and only practicable on the most modest scale. And in default of the creation of new small towns for the displaced workers, these improvements have the effect of accelerating the growth of the city at its edges. The average health of the city will be a little improved, but the cost and time of transport between work and home will be increased, and the contact between the central worker and the countryside further diminished; so that on balance the advantage is much less than is commonly supposed.

THE INTER-WAR HOUSING SCHEMES [1]

The inter-war housing schemes fostered by the Government, with the energetic support of most of the propagandist housing and town-planning societies, produced merely a speeding-up of the previous essentially unsound development. There was no thought of national design.

[1] In the 1918 edition this paragraph was in the future tense. It is with melancholy recognition of my own foresight that I now have to rewrite it in the past tense.

They gave us many more garden suburbs on the fringes of great cities, and some subsidized cottage building in the villages, but there was no attempt to treat the industrial and psychological causes of urban overgrowth and rural decay. None of these schemes went to the root of the matter. They widened rather than bridged the gulf between urban and rural interests which weakens our physical, social, and political life. They perpetuated and even extended the fundamental evils of our urban system and did nothing to arrest the decline of the small towns. For it must be recognized that state-aided housing is free of the economic checks which govern private enterprise. The old system of control by demand and supply, now broken down, was never satisfactory; but it was at least a system, and did distribute houses in some sort of lagging relation to industrial requirements. The inter-war housing schemes were able to evolve no considered principles as a substitute for the lost economic control. Their effect was to promote the growth of existing towns in proportion to the energy of their housing authorities, and to that alone.

The most that can be said for these efforts is that they were better than the previous overcrowding and the wretched surburban development which was universal forty years ago, and still the rule in 1914. If we had to have new suburbs, it was better to have garden suburbs. If cottages had to be added to the towns, it was better that they should be well-planned, pleasing, roomy cottages with adequate garden space, baths, hot water, and other up-to-date conveniences. But no excellence in detail can disguise the fact that all such additions to the towns aggravated a problem which sooner or later had to be faced.

THE SOLUTION

NEW EQUIPMENT IN NEW TOWNS

DURING the first ten years or so after this war we shall have to build a vast number of houses, largely with the aid of national funds. Their erection will coincide with a period of reconstruction, in which our manufacturing, agricultural, educational, and public health methods will come under review. Wide changes will occur. The reorganization of home and foreign trade, the deliberate encouragement of agriculture and certain other basic industries, the impetus to scientific discovery, and the reaccommodation of pre-war businesses, will necessitate the establishment of many new factories, and the development of new plants, new processes, and new kinds of skill. Practically a fresh urban equipment will have to be produced on a colossal scale—houses, roads, factories, all the plant and machinery of industrial life. What is more obvious than to place much of this equipment in new towns designed to secure not only efficiency but the health and happiness of the workers and their families?

The theoretical superiority of the reasonably small town in almost every way can hardly be challenged. It remains to be shown that there is a powerful case for the building of such towns on the garden city model, and how the success of the first two experimental cities of the kind proves the economic and social advantages of the method in practice.

THE GARDEN CITY IDEA

Aspirations to disperse the great cities are as old as dreams of turning back the industrial revolution which

38

caused all the trouble. No progress, however, was made, even by the theorists, until the main innovations of the industrial age were accepted as accomplished facts. Shelley, crying out against the ugliness and cruelty of the urban factory system, was a mere voice in the wind. People heard what he said, made allowances for his youth and talent, and went on building Manchester. All through the nineteenth century our representative men abused the plethoric towns and wept copious tears over the mouldering villages. Nobody seemed to mind. The population streamed incessantly townwards, and ultimately towards a few great cities. By 1831 only about thirty per cent of the people of England and Wales remained engaged in agriculture; by 1901 the proportion had diminished to less than 10 per cent, and by 1937 to 5·6 per cent. This broad change was inevitable, but its extent was excessive. The degree of concentration in a few big cities and town-tracts was also excessive.

Any proposal to divert the stream was derided as fanciful. There was no agency powerful enough to limit the spread of a city or wealthy enough to equip new small towns to meet industrial needs. That intrepid idealist, Robert Owen, inspired by some educational suggestions made as far back as 1695 by John Bellers, the Quaker, was among the first to propose the establishment of model communities to relieve the overcrowded towns. He actually started several industrial villages, but the more ambitious of his schemes foundered under their heavy cargo of revolutionary ideas. The Communist Manifesto of 1848 contained a demand for the 'combination of agriculture with manufacturing industries; and the gradual abolition of the distinction between town and country by a more equable distribution of the population over the country.' But after the efforts of Owen a sort of fatalism settled on practical reformers; they became obsessed with the notion that cities would inevitably grow larger and larger for ever. That fatalistic obsession is not extinct. And although proposals for model communities came up with a certain regularity, none of them had that convincing air of being a 'business proposition' which alone could commend a scheme of such magnitude to the nineteenth century. The discussion, however, went on and came nearer to earth as it progressed.

It was left to Ebenezer Howard and his associates to bring the discussion to the point of an experiment on clearly defined principles.[1] The two Garden Cities, Letchworth, founded in 1904, and Welwyn, founded in 1920, have had a great and widespread influence upon the arts of house design and town planning, but their essential character is still very imperfectly understood by the public. The great progress of the town-planning movement, and the popularity of garden suburbs, have obscured the much more fundamental propositions which Letchworth was designed to test, and Welwyn to re-emphasize.

A FORMULA FOR MODERN TOWNS

The garden city idea will rank as one of the greatest contributions to constructive sociology, because it finds a valid formula for the true relationship of town and country. When we consider the sedulous attention paid by the nineteenth century to the economics of industry and the phenomena of urban growth, it seems remarkable that a suitable formula was so late in making its appearance. The orthodox economists who accepted large-scale production as an irrevocable step in industrial

[1] The experiments were based on a book published in 1898 under the title *To-morrow*, and later reissued as *Garden Cities of To-morrow* by Ebenezer Howard (George Allen & Unwin Ltd).

evolution made no serious attempt to criticize the general character of town structure in the light of that acceptance. All the criticism came from men who were temperamentally in revolt against industrialism, and was consequently dismissed as contrary to the spirit of the age. But as the expansion of great cities, the stagnation or decline of small towns, and the depletion of the countryside were notoriously producing social evils of the gravest kind, surely it would have been no offence against the zeitgeist to ask the simple question: *What, given the modern industrial system, is the best theoretical size for a town?* Yet the question was not asked. It is only within the last few years that economists and town-planning experts have become conscious of its pertinence.

Once the question is asked, it almost answers itself. The town must clearly be large enough to permit of the full division of labour in production and distribution, of power and transport equipment on an efficient scale, and of all the social amenities that people expect of city life. It need be no larger. There are powerful reasons why it should not be larger. And here we come upon the first element of the garden city idea. Just as the requirements of industry and urban society impose a certain minimum of population, so the interests of adequate dwelling-space, public health, agriculture, civic community, and contact with the countryside, impose a maximum. The maximum can be more readily expressed in terms of area than in terms of population; but the two factors are closely linked together, since public health demands a restriction of population-density as well as of area. Agricultural interests would be best served, if it were practicable, by such a distribution of towns as would place the largest area of rural land within convenient reach of them. This also is a limiting factor on size. Now, in order to protect the vital feature of limitation,

the town must be encircled by a belt of open land, wide
enough to possess a distinctively rural character and to
permit of farming on a scale proper to the district. And
in order to keep other towns at arm's length, to maintain
direct contact between urban and rural life, and to permit
of full agricultural productivity, most of this belt of land
must be permanently reserved for farming or non-urban
purposes.

The conception of fixing the scale of the town so as to
promote the best attainable blend of urban and rural
activities is the most characteristic part of the garden
city idea; but it is not sufficient as it stands. The
limitation of size must be safeguarded. And intelligent
design of the town is important. To these ends Howard
made it a feature of his scheme that the whole of the
town land and the necessary minimum of encircling rural
land shall be owned by a public or quasi-public body
capable of carrying out all development. This is the
second element of the garden city idea. The precise legal
form of the ownership is not a fundamental point. The
freehold may be the property of the State, or a municipality, or a trust. What matters is that the land shall
be held and administered under a unified control in the
general interest. This makes possible the building of
the town (or, in the case of an old town, its reformation)
on a plan which has a right regard for every claim—the
needs of manufacture and agriculture, the well-being of
the inhabitants, considerations of natural and artificial
beauty, and the rest of the complex group of urban
interests. If the ownership of the land of a new town is
public the further advantage is gained that the additional
rental values created by the presence of an urban population go to enrich the community.

It is now possible to state the bare elements of the garden
city idea in a brief formula of general applicability—

a scientific constructive prescription which, if this reasoning is sound, ought to influence the development of all industrial towns, new and old:

(a) *A town should be of a population large enough to allow of efficient industrial organization and full social activity; but no larger. The urban area should be limited to a size requisite to house this population well, and should be surrounded by a zone of open land large enough to possess a distinctively rural and agricultural character.*

(b) *The whole of the land, including the urban area and the rural zone, should be owned and administered in the interest of the community.*

APPLICATION OF THE FORMULA

The reduction of this formula to figures and dimensions requires a longer analysis than is possible here. There is little doubt that a population of 30,000 to 50,000 would be ample for most normal industrial purposes; on the present average scale of manufacture it would permit of a very considerable diversity of industry within the town. To accommodate a population of 50,000 well, according to modern town-planning standards, would require an urban area of about 2,000 acres, with an average density of twenty-five persons to the acre, which is about the tolerable maximum density to include work-places, public buildings, shops, and town open spaces. A town of this size, and roughly round in shape, would have a radius of about a mile, which would enable all its industrial workers to be within walking or cycling distance of their work, of the town centre, and of the open country, and an extensive rural community to have easy access to the markets and social attractions of the town.

The requirements of the several interests studied in the garden city formula are thus shown to be consistent one with another. Recognizing that there are variations of taste in urban make-up, and that the liking for comparative simplicity is a legitimate variation, it is convenient to suggest 15,000 as a minimum and 60,000 as a maximum population for light industry towns. Above 40,000 or so the need of internal transport would arise, without substantial compensations. But there will be cases where, unless we change our ideas as to the merits of large-scale industrial units, somewhat larger populations will have to be allowed for. Good economic cause should, however, be shown in any such case in view of the social and civic disadvantages.

A word must be said about the extent of the rural zone. If the whole problem of urban distribution were observed purely from the agricultural standpoint, the importance of a fairly wide spacing out of new towns would be seen. Ten to fifteen miles from centre to centre might be, in the agriculturist's eyes, a reasonable distance for towns of a mile radius; and if a large part of the urban population of Britain had been grouped in this ideal manner the greater part of the present cultivated lands would have been within seven or eight miles of a lively town. We are very far from any such intelligent reorganization as that, and it is academic to discuss it. For the present purpose of formulating a widely applicable policy, all that is possible is the suggestion of a minimum. The rural zone would not fully answer its primary purposes unless its area were at least three times that of the town, and this proportion is accordingly put forward as a practical guide.

PLANNING OF A MODERN TOWN

The corporate ownership of the land enables the town to be laid out on scientific and aesthetic principles, with all its functions duly co-ordinated as the character of the

Graphic Photo Unio

TWO TYPES OF ENVIRONMENT

bove). The substitute for the private garden in a Midland city.
elow). Within five minutes of the factory area of the new town of Welwyn
Garden City.

Studio Li

site suggests. Details of town planning are not an integral part of the garden city idea, but the creation of a new town obviously gives the fullest scope for the application of the art. The grouping of the factories, workshops, and power installations on a specific area to which the dwellings of the workers have some relation, is of primary importance; and great attention must necessarily be paid to the arrangement of railway and canal sidings and other facilities adjacent to the factory sites. Limits should be set to the density of building. Experience has shown that for small houses twelve to the acre is a workable maximum, which allows of good site and house planning and garden plots of manageable size. But the number of buildings to the acre might alternatively be graduated in accordance with the cubic content or floor area of the buildings. And general control must be exercised over plans and elevations, so that anything ugly or extravagant may be excluded, though as much liberty should be left to individual taste as is consistent with this aim. (A very difficult issue which no one has yet fully thought out.)

The New Town Experiments

The practicability of these principles was fully proved by the Letchworth experiment. In this case the planned urban area is two square miles, the rural belt five square miles, and the intended population 35,000. The difficulty of obtaining capital for what was regarded as a visionary scheme hindered progress at first and necessitated some minor compromises; but the essential principles have been adhered to, and the contentions of the founders have been amply proved. The site originally contained three small villages and a few isolated houses in a declining rural district. It was an area in which there was no tendency to spontaneous industrial development. Every service

D

had to be provided *de novo*. Yet Letchworth is now a vigorous industrial town of 20,000 inhabitants. Some of the industries are entirely new; some have migrated from London and other large towns. They are very varied; and they have had at least a normal measure of success. The value of the land has of course greatly increased by the presence of urban activity, and the enterprise is now in a very strong financial position. As the profits of the landowning company are limited to a cumulative five per cent per annum, the local public have a definite interest in its financial success.

Welwyn Garden City, the second of Howard's new towns, was started after the first publication of this book, and I have briefly referred to its history in the introduction. While it was founded to illustrate the same basic principles as Letchworth, it differs widely in many important details, from architectural style to economic organization. And it has a quite different civic climate. I would even say, though it will offend many hide-bound theorists who evolve from their own inner consciousnesses their pictures of what a 'raw new town' must be like, that Letchworth and Welwyn already show, to those who will take the trouble to know them, rich and interesting new variations in the English urban tradition. In nothing is this shown more clearly than in the genial hostility that exists between them. Each has among its citizens passionate enthusiasts and fierce detractors. This is reassuring. Future new towns are certain to vary as widely from Letchworth and Welwyn as these two towns do from each other. It is impossible to impose a stereotyped pattern where the physical background is necessarily different and hundreds of assorted businesses and thousands of personalities are the material. We need not fear, because we discover and apply certain valid principles of urban planning, that thereby we run into

any danger of a dull uniformity. The infinite variability
of topography and of human beings will take care of that.

ADVANTAGES OF A GARDEN CITY

It is now possible to state the realized superiority of
the garden city over the urban types that preceded it.
The workers have better dwellings. Their houses can be
arranged to permit of adequate sunlight and air-space.
Gardens and allotments can be provided adjoining every
house. The factories are within walking distance, and
are more pleasant and healthy places to work in than can
be provided in the crowded towns. The health of the
whole family is better: the rapid change in the appearance of children coming to Letchworth or Welwyn from
London and other large cities is most remarkable. The
infant mortality is exceedingly low; far lower than in any
other industrial town. There are good shops. (I have
not the space to discuss the radically different methods by
which Letchworth and Welwyn dealt with the shopping
problem.) There is a choice of schools and professional
men. The towns are large enough to support a congrega-
tion of every religious body and a branch of every political
society. Nearly all the amenities of city life are available, including above all the sense of vitality and activity.
There are cinemas, dances, sports, swimming baths,
amateur drama, music, lectures, adult education, strikes,
lockouts, elections, demonstrations, clubs—most of the
appurtenances of a full civilized life at the present stage
of human progress. And yet within ten minutes' walk
of the centre of each town is the open country. Neither
Letchworth nor Welwyn has yet attained the population
aimed at as a standard. But the indications are that
35,000 or so would carry an organization satisfying to
almost all people of 'urban' habits.

INDUSTRIAL ADVANTAGES

From the industrial standpoint the advantages of a garden city are that it offers plenty of factory space, railway sidings, gas, water, and power, designed to meet industrial requirements, and at cheap urban rates. In a factory area, planned from the start for industry, it is possible to provide the best types of buildings arranged for convenience and economy of working and good in appearance. Cheap labour is not and should not be available, since the economic saving should rather go to the provision of good housing, garden space, public services, and personal spending power; but a better average standard of workmanship and working enthusiasm is obtainable at the standard rate of wages. The progressive manufacturer realizes that the workers in his factory are more intelligent and efficient when their surroundings are healthy and cheerful. The employer who still fails to grasp this truth is likely to be impervious to any argument based on a thoroughly critical study of industrial facts. The practice and the literature of modern business have finally exploded the theory that cheap labour is generally advantageous as a competitive factor; and the industries of which this is still true are diminishing in number.

The garden city is not in the line of Utopian communities. It is not a scheme for the localized trial of revolutionary self-contained economic systems, though as a field for industrial experiments it offers many advantages. Remaining a part of the commercial system, the garden city collects together and organizes in a scientific manner the most up-to-date methods of production, taking into account not only the conditions of competitive industry, but the well-being of all concerned. The great national and international debate upon the question of industrial control goes on inside the garden city as everywhere else.

MODERN FACTORIES IN A NEW TOWN

A new town will reflect the best architectural standards of its period. The
two factories at Welwyn Garden City, separated in date by fifteen yea
are in different styles, but each has great beauty in its own way. Mc
important still, each is sunny, spaciously sited, surrounded by trees, flowe
and grass, healthy and pleasant to work in, and close to the workers' hom

Whatever the result, whether industry is to be capitalistic or collective, or a mixture of both, efficiency of the kind which is based upon the best labour-saving equipment and a good social and civic life will be desirable. The garden city not only provides for an advance in social organization, but is in itself a factor in the most efficient system of production.

EFFECT ON AGRICULTURE

Not the least interesting of the reactions of the garden city is its effect on the surrounding country. Round about Letchworth and Welwyn the rural belt is largely devoted to the production of milk, vegetables, poultry, and fruit for the needs of the towns, which consume also the produce of their own gardens and small holdings. The value of supplies of perishable foodstuffs close at hand is obvious. The production of vegetables in the town gardens is very great, and is quickly expanded in war-time. The land inside and about the towns is fully cultivated. It is probable that the food production of their whole areas is greater than it was when their sites were purely agricultural. Many farm workers live in the towns. Conversely a large number of men and women of the neighbouring villages cycle to work in the industries and businesses of the towns and share in their social advantages. It is common for families to have some of their members working in the factories and others on the land. Farmers complain that the competition of the industries has raised rural wages. Against this they have a market near at hand for products at better prices.

THE LESSONS OF THE EXPERIMENTS

When further garden cities are built they will be able to profit in many ways by the lessons of the Letchworth and Welwyn experiments. The art of town planning has advanced greatly in the last forty years. It is now possible to estimate with fair accuracy the proportionate areas required for the different organs of the town, and to place them better. Experience also lays stress on the financial importance of rapid development. The initial outlay on roads, sewers, mains, water and gas works, and power plant, is large, though less than in equivalent suburban development; and a full complement of houses and factories must follow quickly if compound interest is not to skim off the advantages of the urban values created. In innumerable details, also, the two experiments provide examples and warnings for the future town-builder. But the main things proved by them are: (1) that the creation of new towns is possible, and (2) the overwhelming economic, sanitary and civic superiority of the garden city over the great town on the one hand or the remote village on the other. In the light of this proof, the continuance of the pre-war drift of things would be nothing less than national suicide by negligence.

THE PROGRAMME

BUILD GARDEN CITIES!

IT will be seen at once that acceptance of the foregoing arguments would have a considerable influence on any national programme of town reconstruction. There is no escape from the logic of the situation. An intelligent policy for Great Britain must include the creation of new small towns on the garden city formula, and the application of the lessons learnt to the existing small towns. The rebuilding of the great cities so as to secure health, efficiency, and civic community is a difficult matter, both in discussion and execution. It is not possible in this little book to deal with the complicated problem of the blitzed areas; of which, however, the author is all too well aware. In many of those areas some loosening-out is badly needed. We cannot, in a crowded city centre, put back all that was there before; and if we could it would be sheer folly to do so. A 'spill-over' has to be provided for. So that a 'new town' policy must accompany the better planning of older areas. With the new towns we can and should begin at once. It has been shown that during the first ten years of peace a vast number of new buildings will be required; that much of the cost of housing has to be borne by the State; that for this and other reasons the State is in a position to guide the distribution of buildings; and that the State is morally bound to find some considered principle of design in the place of the extinct economic checks on town growth. Unless there is a grave fallacy in the reasoning of this book, the practical conclusion is evident. We have to think after this war, as we ought to have thought after the last, not merely of a housing programme, but of a town-building programme. And we must begin the reorganization of our industrial and social system by the establishment of a number of new towns as soon as possible after the termination of the war.

No one can yet say what the rebuilding task may amount to. But it is certain that we shall need new urban equipment of all kinds—factories, houses, shops, and public buildings—for four or five million people. In any case, that is the lowest estimate of the number of people in crowded areas in 1939 who ought to have been provided with work and dwellings in better situations in order to make things comfortable for the millions to be rehoused in the great cities. That would have been a long-term job had there been no war. The war has changed the tempo and character of the process. War, at the same time, accustoms us to large national enterprises. Our resumption of peaceful activities, after what may be a long interval of time, and is certainly a vast derangement of habits and ideas, will have the character of a fresh start in life. Then, if ever, will be the moment to commence the application of great constructive principles. The idea of replanning old cities and building new ones on a national scale will appeal to the imagination of all classes and will draw to its service the best of our intelligence and manual skill. It will appeal in particular to men in the fighting services who want first of all to be with their families again in pleasant homes, but who will also see in new towns a prospect of the healthy conditions and of scope for ambition such as in former times returning soldiers often sought in the newer countries. And, as will be seen later, it has a special interest for business men who understand the necessity for improvements in our manufacturing methods.

CENTRAL ARRANGEMENT AND LOCAL AUTONOMY

If the project is to be taken in hand in conjunction with the deliberate revival of agriculture and the effort to increase industrial efficiency, a leading part must be played by the State. Central organization is essential. It is not impossible that new towns should be built by wealthy syndicates as a commercial speculation, and if done with knowledge, skill, and speed the business would pay, but there are some objections to the method. The development of a city is a social enterprise, and cannot proceed along the best lines unless it has the common good for its aim. Urban values are created by co-operative effort in which the inhabitants play a large part, and should, therefore, benefit the whole community. Moreover, the location of the new cities has to be considered in relation to rural needs; they ought not to be sited, for example, on first-class market-gardening land, though they could with much advantage be near such land. And there are many other considerations in siting. All this demands design, and design implies control, or at least clear guidance.

Subject to these necessities there is much to be gained by the maximum autonomy in matters of planning and details of administration. There is no need for the new cities to be tied to the apron-strings of a grandmotherly government department. Scope for local experiments would foster civic consciousness and emulation, and promote an interesting diversity. Methods will be suggested by which the combination of central design and regional responsibility may be secured.

The situation for the new towns (and choice of existing small towns for expansion) is essentially a matter for central and regional decision after a careful industrial examination of the whole country.

One main factor in deciding situation would be the relationship to railways, roads, and canals, giving suitable access to raw materials, markets, and ports. It can be argued theoretically that the position of cities should govern rather than be ruled by that of the lines of communication. In our highly developed country the position of existing railways, canals, and roads will much influence that of the new cities; nor is there much harm in such influence if the sites are otherwise carefully chosen; conversely, some new road-building would be necessary to serve them. The building of some of the new cities on or near the canal routes is worth investigation, as it might provide the extra incentive needed for the long overdue reform of our inland waterways, which many think is an asset we have neglected.

The Methods of Promotion

The exact means by which the building of new towns should be organized requires consideration from case to case, and only general suggestions are made here. The financial, industrial, administrative, and town-planning data exist, however, in great detail, and can easily be brought together.

It is suggested that the State, through a suitable department—for example, the Ministry of Planning which the Government has promised us—should lay down certain principles upon which new town schemes would be financed, and should invite the co-operation of local authorities, or of building societies, housing organizations, manufacturers, or societies formed for the purpose by public-spirited citizens, in arranging the promotion and management of such schemes. It may be expected that if (on lines to be later sketched) support is promised by the State, the claims of possible sites will at once be argued by local bodies in various areas, and it will be possible to estimate what measure of local driving force is forthcoming. In a case where a satellite town is needed to take the 'spill-over' from the congested parts of a great city, the Corporation of that city might well build the town or take part in its building. Or a county council might be the promoting body. As an alternative, there is much to be said for public utility companies on the model of First Garden City Ltd (the freeholders of Letchworth), which could assume the financial responsibility and act as trustees for the new communities until they develop their own governing machinery.

THE FINANCIAL BASIS

The financial basis of a garden city (as Howard advocated the idea) is that land is acquired at rural value and some of it turned into urban land; the 'betterment,' or extra value, after paying interest on the cost of the site and development, being available for public purposes. Granted rapid development and the proper fixing of ground rents, the surplus is certain. If the State, as financier, could also stimulate speed of growth it would have an excellent investment. But in the very first stages no adequate return is obtainable, so that security of the kind usually demanded by the State on housing schemes is not possible, nor is there at first much local rateable value to be mortgaged. This has been an obstacle in the way of a contribution of State loans on mortgage coupled with private investment under a dividend limit: a form of co-operation which might tap a good deal of public spirit and business ability. In practice the State, especially as it is in the position to encourage industry to settle in the new towns, would have to run a technical risk in waiting for interest on its advances. And it is logical in that case that it should appoint some directors of the public utility company. When the initial stages were passed, and urban values had begun to accrue, the State might recede from its part in the control and become an ordinary mortgagee, so long as the principles laid down were duly observed. The annual surplus might be divided between the State and the cities.

This question of immediate security has to be mentioned, but stress upon it would imply a financial timidity in the State which would be the ruin of any commercial concern. Moreover, the national value of such an investment cannot be measured merely in terms of improved ground rents.

Conditions of State Support

Suitable sites having been selected, the land would be compulsorily acquired either by the appropriate ministry or by a local authority, and vested in or leased to the local authority or the local garden city trust. In the case of the local authority the State would advance at the current rate of interest the capital cost of developing the towns, including all necessary improvement to transport facilities and the equipment of gas, water, and power plants; and the cost of factories and other buildings so far as these were to be built by the town. Housing would be financed in the ordinary way. In the case of a trust or public utility company the advance might be ninety per cent of development costs, and some such conditions as the following might be imposed:

1. Development to be on garden city principles, including (a) freehold to be retained, and ground rents of shop premises reviewed at stated intervals; or shops built and let at rack rents only; (b) town area and rural belt to be defined; (c) houses nowhere to be built in excess

Architects: C. H. Elsom & H. Stone   *Studio Lisa*

A NEW TOWN CENTRE

(*Above*). The municipal offices in the new town of Welwyn Garden City.
(*Below*). A shopping and business street.   This picture shows, among other things, that we can have architectural harmony, and dignity, without constriction of space.

Architect: Louis de Soissons, F.R.I.B.A.   *Studio Lisa*

of a stated density—expressed perhaps in floor-space per acre; (d) the trust to employ qualified officers for planning and control of building and external design.

2. The original town plan and later variations to be submitted to the departmental town-planners for criticism and suggestion; full local control, however, being retained, subject to observance of national standards. (This seems to be the best way to avoid blunders of inexperience without stereotyping or delaying development.)

3. Dividend on share capital to be limited. The State to have a percentage of any surplus after payment of dividend. Balance to be used for approved public purposes.

4. The State (or the financing local authority) to have the right to nominate one-third of the Board of Management.

In the case of a new town directly built by a municipality some of these conditions are inapplicable. Others might be modified after full consideration. They are put forward neither as an irreducible minimum nor as an idealistic maximum; but simply as a suggestion of the kind of measures necessary to safeguard the vital elements of the project.

It is not easy to estimate how much capital would be required from the State under this scheme. The cost of developing one entirely new town of 50,000 population (at pre-war prices) might vary from one to ten million pounds, according to the amount of building done by the estate itself. Part of the building cost would be expended by manufacturers, builders, and others. In any case, if new towns are not established, a like capital expenditure on development, buildings, and plant will still occur somewhere or other; the scheme does not entail any extra draft on the financial resources of the nation. It may or may not require a greater proportion of the capital to pass through the hands of public authorities; that is a matter of the financial mechanism chosen for all forms of development. No extra charge on the revenue is involved. Development in the new towns will most assuredly not cost more than redevelopment catering for the same numbers of people in an old centre. What happened between the wars shows that it is likely to cost much less.

Some legislation would be necessary to empower the Treasury to make loans to local authorities and corporate bodies for town development and purposes accessory thereto—including expenditure upon lands, roads, buildings, industrial services, and means of transport—and to give local authorities the right to invest in and control trust associations, or to exercise the powers of public companies. There are, of course, numerous partial precedents for such legislation.

THE ERECTION OF FACTORIES AND SHOPS

The prosperity of the new towns will rest primarily upon their utility as centres of productive industry. The provision of factories and factory plant must, therefore, claim first consideration. Promoters of new industries, as well as many established firms who are awake to the need of an increased output after the war, may be expected to observe that the conditions offered by the proposed garden cities are as nearly as possible ideal manufacturing conditions. The new towns should combine with their various natural advantages of situation (which will have been duly weighed in advance) a unique series of artificial advantages arising out of the fact that they can be specially and expertly designed for modern methods of production. A manufacturer taking a site in one of these towns will be able to erect at the minimum cost a factory in precise accord with the organization of his business. He will not be hampered by insufficient space either in his original plant or in his provision for enlargement, since he will obtain ample land at a small annual rental with security of tenure. His charges for interest on cost of building, fire insurance, local rates, lighting and ventilating, and in many cases for heating and air-washing, will be lower than in the big towns; while as against the country factory he will have a more flexible labour supply, proper fire protection, and the use of municipal power, gas, water, and drainage at rates cheaper than any at which he could provide them for himself. Railway, and in some cases, canal sidings with their appropriate gear will be at his factory doors. Freightage costs cannot be compared without reference to the exact situation of the new towns and the respective bulk of materials and finished products; but it is certain that numerous industries formerly stationed close to their markets or the sources of their supplies could be re-established in an intermediate position without increase of total transportation costs. It should also be noted that in some of the most highly capitalized and organized industries (such as light machine engineering) freightage is small compared with other cost factors. Especially is this the case with the manufactures centralized in big towns, and with many of the industries which will have to be established afresh after the war.

A productive factor compelling more and more attention is the housing and general welfare of the workers in industry. Modern business executives are now well alive to the industrial value of good conditions, though they have sometimes been misguided in the application of their theories—through a failure to realize that the workers want social liberty and opportunity as much as they want pleasant physical surroundings. There is no doubt whatever that the future is with those businesses which understand and provide in advance for both demands. And here the new towns will challenge all competitors. Men demobilized from the forces will have been shaken out of old routines and will be critical of the confused city, its long journeys, its crowded dwellings and workshops. They and their fellow workers will very reasonably ask for the best possible town conditions, seeing that in any case most of them will not simply return to a familiar scene. Unquestionably the best and most intelligent of the workers will be strongly attracted to modern and lively towns, and once there will wish to remain. In such towns, businesses should be able to keep together their selected and trained staffs more permanently than in cities where there are no local ties or in country places where for the typical urban worker the life is unvaried and dull.

It may be anticipated that many of the factories in the new towns will be built by firms who intend to occupy them. In fact it is possible that some manufacturers who realize the urgent need for improved industrial methods will take the lead in the promotion of schemes for new towns in districts suitable for their own businesses. But the town authorities themselves should be prepared to build model factories to be let on rental; and it would facilitate this if adequate capital were provided by the State or other agencies for the purpose. Much business enterprise after the war will be of necessity somewhat experimental, owing to the widespread dislocation of foreign commerce and the difficulty of predicting the channels in which trade will finally settle down. Bold experiment will be a condition of industrial adaptation. If British industry waits until the new channels are fixed before selecting its own lines of activity, British industry will be too late. The new towns can do much to facilitate the requisite degree of enterprise by providing suitable factory premises, designed in the first instance for a special industry, but capable of future modification if the original business is not successful. Many industries with more calculable prospects but limited capital will also be induced to commence operations in the new towns if buildings are provided for them.

Sectional or divisible factories, with central heating, convenient loading arrangements, fixtures for power transmission, and light partitions, should be provided for novel industries which can begin on a small scale, or for larger businesses not fully convinced of their own prospects or of the suitability of a garden city location. In such buildings a business would lease as much floor space as it needed for the time being, with the opportunity of expanding its accommodation when required. Many firms beginning in this way, and gradually perfecting their organization, would ultimately build their own premises in the town. Workshops should be built for minor industries, as much care being given to them in matters of situation and design as to the larger factories; for in spite of the increase in the scale of certain types of manufacture, small businesses will continue to play a very valuable part in the economic system. In fine, it should be one of the chief aims of the new towns to meet the case of businesses of all kinds, whether they are small or large, steady or fluctuating; so that as far as possible they may be provided with the right amount of floor space and equipment for their current needs, and the waste of establishment charges, like all other wastes, kept down to the minimum.[1]

Practical economists will at once perceive the immense scope there is for municipal organization in matters of

---

[1] This conception of a 'trading estate' as part of town development, first put forward in the 1918 edition of this book, was adopted at Welwyn with marked success.

E

this kind, irrespective of basic changes in the general industrial system.

Similar principles may be applied to the erection of shops, stores, and other business premises. Retail and service businesses will easily be attracted to new towns. They will be all the more ready to do so if their interests are protected by the careful planning of the business area, and the limitation of the number of shops and stores to a reasonable number, consistent with good service and the interests of the consumers. The town should possess sufficient resources to supplement private activity to whatever extent the common welfare of the inhabitants may suggest.[1]

HOUSING IN THE GARDEN CITIES

Housing might be undertaken by the town-promoting authority or trust itself; or by controlled public utility societies (debarred from profit-making in the same way), with provision for transfer to the local authority if and when required. For this purpose State loans should be granted to the trust or to the societies on very favourable terms. To what extent State housing subsidies will be necessary after this war cannot yet be predicted. It is vital, however, that subsidy policy shall favour the building of good houses in the small towns rather than tenements in overcrowded great cities. Many houses would no doubt continue to be erected by housing companies, builders, building societies, and prospective residents. The garden city building regulations should

---

[1] This policy also was developed at Welwyn—to an even greater extent than this book originally proposed. The financial importance of the ownership of shop buildings by a progressive estate cannot be exaggerated. Municipalities engaged in redevelopment of city centres, as well as those promoting new towns, would do well to make a close study of the Welwyn methods and experience.

insist on good architectural design, a certain minimum of cubic content, floor and window space, etc., the provision of baths, hot water, and all other indispensable fittings, and sound construction, but should permit of as much variety as possible in the application of good principles. This may lead to a few eccentricities, but occasional freaks will be better than a dead sameness.

NEIGHBOURHOOD CO-OPERATION

To the extent that domestic or neighbourhood co-operation is desired, new towns, with their completely new and planned residential areas, will be good places for trying it out in various forms. The problem is not a simple one. Some married women who have found congenial employment during the war will be reluctant to return to whole-time housekeeping. On the other hand, keeping house for a family is important work; and there are many signs of a new and modern re-emphasis of family idealism—with which the wholesale employment of married women in industry and business, necessary as it is in war-time, does not well consort. The solution for most people will not be found in co-operative housekeeping, but rather in the better equipment of the individual family home, coupled perhaps with group heating and hot water supplies and with some development of small local restaurants and of nursery schools, which would supplement rather than replace the home. Where entirely new residential areas are being created, there is room for experiment on these lines. But it would be a mistake to plan for a whole-sale change of fundamental family habits. These external accessories to the family life are more likely to follow a rise in industrial productivity than to be a means of attaining it. They must not be purchased at the expense of space for family living or the privacy of the family house and garden. In this matter the strong instinctive prejudices of most normal people are in tune with the biological interests of the race, and we could only override or divert them at our peril. It is a very interesting problem: to devise neighbourhood services and associations that will enrich family life without weakening its mainsprings.

CIVIC DIRECTORS

Efforts should be made from the very beginning to associate the residents of the town with the complex business of its development by means of the direct election of a few members of the body taking charge of development. This will add to the vitality of the place, safeguard what is after all the most important interest, and fan the spark of civic pride.[1] It is hardly possible for a new garden city, consisting in its early days largely of anticipations, to feel a social unity in its sacred past. Its unity, if felt at all, will reside in its present activities and in its future promise. The people will look forward rather than back. They will make local tradition rather than live upon it. But they can only attain full consciousness of the complex process of the creation of the town by participating in the discussion and control of its development. In the great towns local tradition has died out, either because there is no present activity to keep it alive, or because they are too large and undemocratic to form and hold common ideas. The new towns will have all the resources of modern science and industry to call upon, and the inspiration of a great common de-

[1] This experiment was tried in the early days of Welwyn Garden City, with considerable success, and its subsequent abandonment has been a loss to the civic sense of the town.

sign; and if the townsfolk are from the first fully conscious of that design they will already feel themselves to be citizens of no mean city.

EFFECT ON THE STATE

It is not too much to say that the construction of a number of new garden cities, with the stimulus of emulation added to the interest of a great national enterprise, would in a measure quicken the democratic life of the whole community. A great deal is written nowadays about civic consciousness and so on, which practical men are apt to dismiss as the mere inflation of language. But it is a powerful reagent which causes the release of all this gas. War has made men feel the inspiration of a common disinterested activity and the worth of public service. And inspiration now employed for destructive ends can be carried over into constructive industrial and political concerns. There is already a strong disposition to consider our institutions liquefied so that they may be cast into a shape which will suit the new ideas. The danger is that the conflict for control will dwarf everything; for in the industrial sphere the masses of people have little power over the determination of new forms, and in political matters our chief towns are too large and formless for effective democracy or civic consciousness to be practicable. Towns such as are here proposed will be an outlet for constructive energies and schools for public spirit, precisely because they are new and small.

They may also provide a pattern for the revival of existing country towns, many of which are possible centres for modern industry. Those that are on important highways, railway lines, rivers, or canals, already possess the chief qualification for industrial development under present conditions. But in some cases their public services need to be brought up to date and their industrial equipment remodelled; processes which call for heavy capital expenditure, but which, if well carried out, would be remunerative in themselves and of inestimable value to the country as a whole. If the small towns could regain their vigour the development of a real national cultural life would be possible. The arts which require capital and organization, such as the drama, opera, and orchestral music, are at present only accessible to the residents of a few great towns, and beyond the means of most of them. If the typical unit of civilization were the small town, as on every ground it should be, or even if there were a few score of lively small towns with the needful equipment, all these co-operative arts could be oragnized on a circulating basis. At present the only art which has as much as a national scope is the art of the cinema, and that is cosmopolitan—simply because the transport of films is cheap, and their exhibition is therefore within the means of very small towns. But the cinema (important as it is and still more valuable as it may become) cannot be considered a sufficient system of culture in itself.

Our garden cities and country towns should have comfortable theatres and concert-rooms as inevitably as churches, schools, and public halls, and many of these buildings might be municipally owned. To such circumstances the organized arts would readily adapt themselves by eliminating extravagant settings and high prices, which are the result of present urban conditions. Only a tiny fraction of the city workers can afford to be regular patrons of the theatre, and these go as beggars to the feast provided for the stalls, while the provincial tour of to-day is broken meat from the same board. If the organization were based on the demand of lively small towns, really good performances would come within reach of the whole

THE COUNTRY BELT OF A NEW TOWN

Letchworth Agricultural Belt : Studio Lisa

'No festering and wretched suburb anywhere, but clean and busy street within and the open country without . . . so that from any part of the city perfectly fresh air and grass and sight of far horizon might be reachable in a few minutes' walk.' —John Ruskin (quoted by Ebenezer Howard in *Garden Cities of To-morrow*).

population—including, be it specially noted, the workers of the agricultural districts. A closer linking of amateur drama, music, and other forms of social art with the professional organization of the same arts would be a strength to both.

It would be possible also at a comparatively small cost in buildings to spread more widely the advantages of other branches of culture. Libraries, picture galleries, and museums, no less than institutions for advanced education and scientific research, could be organized into a truly national system with branches within the reach of all.

Relation to Rural Reform

In a number of areas rural revival would be aided by the creation of new towns and redevelopment of existing small towns. They will tend to increase the output of agricultural produce at points nearer to the producers. To that extent they will provide a sounder economic basis for good village housing, increase the stability of the neighbouring rural economy, and thereby aid further progress. Where sub-standard lands are to be reclaimed or graded up, and rural population therefore increased, the introduction of new industrial centres, either entirely new foundations or based on existing villages, might be conceived as a method of securing a partially balanced local development, and might well help to carry the cost of electric power supplies to the farming areas.

The Future of the Great City

These proposals have not dealt directly with the future of existing large towns, but it is obvious that their adoption would check suburban growth, inasmuch as a good deal of new construction would be transferred to the new garden cities and the smaller existing towns. If we were capable of or desired a thorough-going application of modern planning principles we should re-plan most of the old towns and reorganize the vast town-tracts into federal groups of garden cities separated by parks or gardens or small rural belts; preserving (or rather rescuing) much that is historic and beautiful in the more ancient central districts. All rebuilding should conform to new plans as the old houses wear out and leases fall in; and so the noble and healthy towns of the future would grow gradually out of the disorder of the present. This possibility was alluded to rather despairingly in the first edition of this book. The 'blitzing' of some of the most crowded business and dwelling-house areas in great cities does, however, give opportunities here and there of large-scale replanning and opening-out. There are difficulties about compensation and rateable value; difficulties which can hardly be surmounted unless areas needing drastic replanning first became public or quasi-public property. Even a partial replanning and a limitation of the number of houses per acre would, in default of that condition, present similar difficulties. But sooner or later this great problem must be faced if life is to be made worth living for the urban population; and the fierce misfortunes of the present do seem to give us the opportunity.

A project to transform Bermondsey into a milk farm would be dismissed as wildly daring.[1] But it is far more daring—indeed it is positively reckless—to rebuild Bermondsey piecemeal with its huddled excess of houses; which is what we should inevitably have done in due course had disaster not come to shake us out of our short-

---

[1] I leave this sentence as it was, though I now think I was unfair in picking on Bermondsey, and count myself undeservedly lucky in that I was not censured by that lively and fairly democratic locality.

sighted practicality. When we realize the damage to
health and human values of which our overcrowded
town areas are capable, we shall know that what we took
for moderation and common sense was self-destructive
folly; and what we took for Utopian dreaming is a stern
practical necessity. The inexorable claim of national
health and the rising demand for a pleasant environment
for all workers are the forces which will ultimately tri-
umph over the smaller vested interests and loosen out
and reduce the old urban agglomerations. In the mean-
time, though we have not been wise enough to pull down
any but the most unhealthy parts of our towns, we already
feel that so far as they have been destroyed we shall
not be foolhardy enough to rebuild them in their old
form. If we did not think it 'practicable' to reduce and
replan our overgrown cities, at least we now see that we
must not by sheer indifference let them expand still
further. A constructive alternative is now clearly
before us.

A Great Constructive Proposal [1]

The creation of garden cities and the revivification of
our smaller towns will give a far better return to the State
in health, happiness, public spirit, and efficiency than any
other method of rebuilding Britain. Merely to scatter
millions of dwellings in our suburbs and villages, wherever
a chance economic demand occurred, as we did between
the two wars, was a feeble and planless proceeding. It
meant that a colossal national enterprise was undertaken
without national consideration or design, and in total
disregard of some of the most vital factors. The nation

[1] I have left this enthusiastic wind-up very nearly as in the 1918
edition, merely changing the second and third sentences into the past
tense. Acquired habits of grave understatement would prevent me
from such eloquence now. But every word of it is true.

is now, as it was after the last war, in the position of a man regarding a runaway vehicle; there is nothing for it between cowardice and courage. Again to neglect this opportunity would be ignominious; to seize it would be glorious. No more inspiring task can be imagined than the provision for millions of our people of the best physical environment that modern art and industry can produce.

What a dramatic opening for the era of international reconstruction—Britain, which led the world to industrialism, now showing the way to a system in which industrial wealth is compatible with a sane, natural, and cultured life for all! And what an impulse it will give to the solution of the major problems of society! The great questions of income and control now underlying the industrial and political conflicts of every nation cannot be solved by town planning, but they can be profoundly modified. If a great number of town dwellers secure the inalienable advantages of comfort in their houses, beauty and grace in their surroundings, sunlight, fresh air, health, and a share of civic power; if many more rural workers have access to the social pleasures and opportunities of lively towns; if to a greater extent people of all classes or functions in town and country are brought together and come to understand the interests of each other; then vital political issues will be immensely clarified, and the rise of numerous groups of alert and responsible citizens will quicken national progress in every sphere.

SHORT BOOK LIST

HOWARD, EBENEZER, *Garden Cities of To-morrow*, 1898. Reissued by Geo. Allen & Unwin Ltd, 1914, 2*s*. (now out of print).

PURDOM, C. B., *The Building of Satellite Towns*. J. M. Dent & Sons Ltd, 1925, 25*s*.

ABERCROMBIE, PATRICK, *Town and Country Planning*. Home University Library. Oxford University Press, 1933, 3*s*.

MUMFORD, LEWIS. *The Culture of Cities*. Secker & Warburg, 1938, new edition 1941, 15*s*.

MCALLISTER, GILBERT and ELIZABETH G., *Town and Country Planning*. Faber & Faber, 1941, 12*s*. 6*d*.

TOWNDROW, F. E. (ed.), *Replanning Britain*, being a summarized report of the Oxford Conference of the Town and Country Planning Association. Spring, 1941. Faber & Faber, 1941, 7*s*. 6*d*.

OSBORN, F. J., *Overture to Planning*. (Rebuilding Britain Series, No. 1). *The Land and Planning*. (Rebuilding Britain Series, No. 7). Faber & Faber, 1941, 1*s*. each.

Report of Royal Commission on Distribution of Industrial Population. (The 'Barlow Report.') Cmd. 6153. H.M. Stationery Office, 1940, 5*s*.

Town and Country Planning: Quarterly Journal. Town and Country Planning Association. 1*s*. (5*s*. yearly).

MADE AT
THE·TEMPLE
PRESS

LETCHWORTH
ENGLAND